C000097624

Inchmahome Priory

Richard Fawcett

Edited by Chris Tabraham
Illustrated by Michelle McCluskie and David Simon
Photography by Historic Scotland Photographic Unit
Produced by Roy Stewart Print Services
Printed in Scotland by Buccleuch Printers Ltd. Hawick

First published by HMSO 1986
This revised edition first published by Historic Scotland 1995
Reprinted 1998
Crown Copyright © Historic Scotland 1995
ISBN 1 900168 02 2

Introduction

"Those giant boughs that wave around
My aged hoary head,
Were then the tenants of the ground
Where walked the royal maid."

(FROM REVEREND W M STIRLING'S POEM
INSCHEMACHAME, COMPOSED IN 1815.

THE ROYAL MAID IS MARY, QUEEN OF SCOTS,
AND THE PRIORY IS THE NARRATOR)

Set on the largest of three islands in the Lake of Menteith, against the backdrop of the Menteith Hills, the priory of Inchmahome is among the most attractive of Scotland's medieval religious houses. It is surrounded by a variety of trees and in springtime coloured by daffodils and rhododendrons, and the Lake is home to many birds, including great-crested grebes, geese, herons and swans. This is Scotland's only 'lake' rather than 'loch', and, in severe winters when thick enough ice covers it, curling matches are held - the Grand Match between the north and south of Scotland was last held here in 1979.

The priory was founded in about 1238 for a small community of Augustinian canons, by one of the great magnates of the period, Walter Comyn, earl of Menteith. Towards the end of its life, the priory received one of its most distinguished visitors, the infant Mary, Queen of Scots, who was sent to Inchmahome in 1547 for safety when an English army invaded Scotland. Although the priory church and its associated buildings are now only seen in fragmentary state, enough still remains to make it possible to understand how their arrangement reflected the way of life of the canons whom they were designed to house.

Inchmahome Priory and the Lake of Menteith.

The Story of Inchmahome Priory

THE FOUNDATION

In founding the priory of Inchmahome for a community of Augustinian canons, Walter Comyn, earl of Menteith, hoped to ensure the salvation of his soul through the perpetual prayers of the canons and by virtue of his good work in founding a house for men of God. It was fitting for a great family to have a religious community on its estates, for it underlined both the family's importance and their piety as well as providing a dynastic burial place. Permission to found the priory was granted in 1238 by the bishop of Dunblane. A proportion of the revenues of the parishes of Leny and of Inchmahome itself were immediately appropriated to the new priory, and those of Kilmadock and Linlathan were also eventually devoted to its needs.

The new priory was built on the largest of the three islands in the Lake of Menteith, which was itself at the heart of the ancient province of Menteith. There seems to have been a church on the island before the priory was founded, since there is a documentary reference to a parson of 'insula Macholem' in about 1210. Earl Walter's chief reason for placing his new priory on this island was probably because of its closeness to one of his principal residences. The island adjacent to Inchmahome, Inchtalla, has the remains of an imposing courtyard house of the earls of Menteith and, although much of it is later than the priory, there is likely to have been a residence on the island from at least the time of Earl Walter.

In choosing a community of Augustinian canons for a site where there was already a parish church, Earl Walter would have been conscious that parish and community of canons could operate to mutual advantage in a way which would not have been possible with a house of monks.

The exterior of the choir from the north east, showing the fine grouping of five lancets in the east window.

THE AUGUSTINIAN CANONS

Inherent in Christianity is an ascetic strand of thought which encouraged the more devout souls to live at a distance from what they saw as the snares of the world. For some a solitary existence as hermits was necessary, but more commonly a form of disciplined coexistence as monks was sought by those who felt the need to pursue spiritual perfection. The advantages of such a closely regulated existence, in which personal possessions were renounced, also came to be seen as having benefits for groups of ordained clergy serving major churches. From the middle years of the eleventh century, it was increasingly felt that a formal rule should be followed if such a way of life was to attain sufficient coherence. The basis for a rule was found in the writings of St Augustine of Hippo, who died in 430, and groups of clergy who formed such communities came to be known as Augustinian canons. They were also often known as Black Canons from the colour of their clothing. Their order was formally recognized in about 1059 and introduced into Scotland around 1120.

Although their life was similar to that of monks, they were an essentially priestly order; but they were less strictly enclosed than most monastic orders and were thus able to serve as parish priests, particularly at their own churches. Perhaps another attraction of the Augustinian canons to potential founders was their flexibility. Although a number of Scottish houses of the order, including Holyrood, Jedburgh and St Andrews, grew to great size, others were quite small and undemanding of resources on the part of their founders.

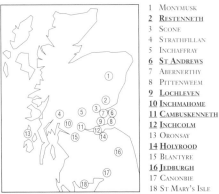

1 MONYMUSK
2 RESTENNETH
3 SCONE
4 STRATHFILLAN
5 INCHAFFRAY
6 ST ANDREWS
7 ABERNERTHY
8 PITTENWEEM
9 LOCHLEVEN
10 INCHMAHOME
11 CAMBUSKENNETH
12 INCHCOLM
13 ORONSAY
14 HOLYROOD
15 BLANTYRE
16 JEDBURGH
17 CANONBIE
18 ST MARY'S ISLE

An Augustinian canon, depicted in William Dugdale's Monasticon Anglicanum.

The Augustinian houses in Scotland, indicating in underlined type those in the care of Historic Scotland.

THE EARLDOM OF MENTEITH

Although Menteith was one of the great provinces of medieval Scotland, relatively little is known of its earls before the thirteenth century. In 1233-4 the earldom passed to the powerful Comyn family when Walter Comyn married Isabel, countess of Menteith in her own right. It was Walter who founded Inchmahome Priory in about 1238, and he died 20 years later. Unfortunately, his countess came to be suspected of having been implicated in the death of her husband, and a struggle for the earldom ensued, in which the chief claimants were Walter's nephew, John, and Walter Stewart, whose wife appears to have been a cousin of Countess Isabel. Walter's claim was ultimately successful, and eventually, in 1285, the lands of the earldom were divided between Walter Stewart and William, the great-nephew of Earl Walter Comyn, with Walter retaining the title. The title remained with his family for several generations.

In 1361 the earldom was acquired by Robert Stewart, a younger son of Robert II, through marriage to Margaret Graham, the widowed countess of that time. Robert Stewart was later created duke of Albany, and he built the mighty castle at Doune (now in Historic Scotland's care); he was also to be governor of Scotland from 1406 until his death in 1420. In 1425, most of the Menteith lands passed to the Crown. The title was later granted to Malise Graham and remained with the Graham family into the seventeenth century. In 1632 Earl William suffered royal disfavour when a claim was made that he had a greater right to the throne than Charles 1. He was consequently reduced to the lesser earldom of Airth.

The double effigy of Walter Stewart, earl of Menteith, who died in about 1295, and his countess.

The mighty castle of Doune, situated 9 miles (15 km) east of Inchmahome, built about 1400 for Robert Stewart, first duke of Albany and earl of Menteith and Fife, as his chief stronghold of the earldom of Menteith.

THE LIFE OF THE COMMUNITY

The chief function of any community of canons or monks was the *opus dei*, the work of God. This varied according to the time of year, but essentially it consisted of a series of eight services, known as the hours, which were spread throughout the day, starting at around half past one in the morning. There were also communal and private masses to be celebrated each day. Much of the rest of the day was spent in reading, contemplation, tending the priory's gardens and orchards, or catching fish. Those canons who were officers of the community had their own tasks. The cellarer, for example, looked after the provisions, the sacrist maintained the furnishings and vestments required for the church services, and the infirmarian supervised the old and infirm canons.

A religious community, which was a landholding body with a prominent place in the feudal hierarchy, also had a more public aspect. The prior was expected to play his part as one of the great men of the kingdom. In 1296 the first recorded prior, Adam, swore allegiance to King Edward I of England. Robert the Bruce paid at least three visits to the priory, in 1306, 1308 and 1310, for he signed documents on those occasions. In 1358 there was another important visit, by the future Robert II.

THE LATER HISTORY OF THE PRIORY

By the early sixteenth century the revenues of Inchmahome were apparently regarded as ripe for picking. In 1508 an apparently unsuccessful attempt was made to allocate them to the Chapel Royal at Stirling, while in 1536 there seems to have been a bid to unite the priory with the abbey of Jedburgh, a sister Augustinian house. But by that time the priory was controlled by the Erskine family, who evidently intended to guard this source of income.

A factor which contributed to the decline in monastic standards in the later Middle Ages was a growing trend of appointing commendators as heads of abbeys and priories. These were royal appointees who were not members of the religious orders and who often had little interest in ensuring that monastic life was pursued with any zeal. Inchmahome was granted to Robert, master of Erskine, in 1529, and he effectively made it an hereditary possession. After his death fighting the English at the Battle of Pinkie in September 1547, the office passed to his brother John, who eventually also held the commendatorships of Cambuskenneth and Dryburgh Abbeys.

A depiction of a service in a monastery over the body of a founder. Although this painting does not show Augustinian canons, it gives a good idea of the interior of a medieval monastic choir, with the high altar as the chief focus, and the stalls along the flanks. (Courtesy of the Trustees of the British Museum.)

This seal of the priory, showing the Virgin holding the infant Jesus, was attached to a document of 1562 recording the grant of a yearly pension to John, Lord Erskine, later earl of Mar.

MARY, QUEEN OF SCOTS

The state of uncertainty following the Battle of Pinkie led, that September, to Inchmahome receiving one of its most famous visitors, Mary, Queen of Scots. Inchmahome was a natural choice, not only because it was an island sanctuary but also because its commendator was the son of Mary's guardian, Lord Erskine.

Mary was only four years old when she and her mother, the dowager Queen, Mary of Guise, were sent from Stirling Castle to the island for their own safety. According to legend, the infant Mary began her studies and practised gardening on the island, but her age and the fact that she was here for only three weeks make these accomplishments unlikely. It is not known which of the priory buildings she occupied, but the prior's residence in the west range is the most likely place.

Mary, Queen of Scots, who stayed in the priory in 1547. The following year she sailed to France, where, in 1558, she married the Dauphin Francis. This portrait by Clouet was painted shortly before her return to Scotland in 1561. (Courtesy of the National Galleries of Scotland.)

THE END OF THE PRIORY

By the time of the Reformation in 1560 the priory housed about 11 canons, and those who so wished were allowed to remain in the priory after it had been secularised. In 1604 and 1606 the priory estates along with those of the abbeys of Dryburgh and Cambuskenneth were formally granted to the Erskine family as a lordship for the second earl of Mar. Inchmahome and Dryburgh were acquired by the marquis of Montrose towards the end of the seventeenth century, perhaps around the same time that he acquired the Menteith estate. The priory was placed in State care by the sixth duke of Montrose in 1926.

A view of the west front of the priory, from W M Stirling's
Notes on the Priory of Inchmahome, *1815.*

A Short Tour of

1. NAVE

FOR THE USE OF LAY FOLK ATTENDING
SERVICES. THE ORNATE WEST FRONT
HAS A PROCESSIONAL DOORWAY AT ITS
CENTRE. INSIDE, AN ARCADE OF FOUR
ARCHES OPENED INTO A NORTH AISLE,
WITH A BELL TOWER SLOTTED INTO
THE WEST BAY. ORIGINALLY A SCREEN
SEPARATED NAVE FROM CHOIR, AND THE
MAIN ALTAR IN THE NAVE WAS SET
AGAINST THE SCREEN.

2. CHOIR

RESERVED FOR THE CANONS
ATTENDING SERVICES. A FINE ARCHED
WINDOW WITH FIVE LANCETS AT THE
EAST END LIT THE HIGH ALTAR.
MOULDED ARCHES GRACE THE *PISCINA*
(BASIN) AND *SEDILIA* (SEATS). A DOORWAY
IN THE NORTH WALL LED TO THE
SACRISTY, WHERE EQUIPMENT USED AT
THE SERVICES WAS STORED.

3. CLOISTER

A RECTANGULAR COURT SURROUNDED
BY THE MAIN DOMESTIC BUILDINGS.
AROUND THE CLOISTER A CORRIDOR
LINKED THE BUILDINGS AND THE NAVE
OF THE CHURCH. ALONG THE SOUTH
AND NORTH SIDES THE WALK HAD ITS
OWN ROOF, BUT ON THE WEST AND
PART OF THE EAST SIDE IT WAS BUILT
INTO THE RANGES OF ROOMS.

hmahome Priory

4. EAST RANGE

CONTAINS THE CHAPTER HOUSE AND WARMING HOUSE ON THE GROUND FLOOR AND ORIGINALLY THE DORMITORY ABOVE. THE LATRINE BLOCK IS AT THE SOUTH END.

5. CHAPTER HOUSE

THE BUSINESS ROOM, USED FOR A DAILY MEETING OF THE CANONS. STILL INTACT WITH A VAULTED CEILING AND A STONE BENCH LINING THE WALLS. IT WAS LATER CONVERTED INTO A MAUSOLEUM FOR LORD KILPONT AND NOW CONTAINS SOME FINE GRAVESTONES AND EFFIGIES.

6. SOUTH RANGE

A RUINED RANGE WHICH CONTAINED THE REFECTORY (DINING HALL).

7. WEST RANGE

A RUINED RANGE WHICH CONTAINED STORE ROOMS ON THE GROUND FLOOR AND THE PRIOR'S LODGING ABOVE.

Artist's bird's-eye view of the priory from the south-east.

The Priory as a Place of Worship

THE CHURCH

*I*nchmahome conformed to the normal layout of a monastery. The largest and most important building was, of course, the church, which was placed towards the north of the site where it would not deny light to the other parts of the complex. These other parts were ranged along the three sides of an open rectangular space flanking the church, known as the cloister, around the perimeter of which ran covered corridors, or walks, to connect the various buildings. Parts of the cloister ranges can still be seen, although nothing survives of the other buildings which might be expected to have spread around it. Some, such as barns, stables, smithies and brew-houses, may have been on the mainland; but others, such as the infirmary for the old and sick monks, would almost certainly have been on the island itself.

The church appears to have been among the first parts of the priory to have been built. As with most churches built for communities of monks or canons, it is made up of two distinct parts, the nave to the west and the choir to the east.

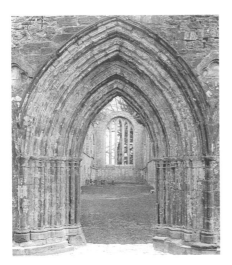

The processional doorway in the west front.

THE NAVE

The **west gable** was the great show-front of the priory church and, despite its relatively small scale, it must have formed an impressive entrance. At the lower level is a fine **processional doorway**, with four orders of finely moulded arches carried on equally rich groupings of engaged shafts. Flanking the doorway is a blind arcade of two arches on each side, with decorative foiled figures between their heads. At the upper level was a large window which appears to have been subdivided into three lights.

Looking into the nave from the north east. The bell tower is on the right, and part of the arcade dividing the aisle from the nave survives next to it.

The **nave** was intended to serve more than one function. The canons passed through it in procession to the choir at certain services, and lay-folk, for whom it may have acted as their parish church, entered from the door in the north wall to attend their services. Its design appears to have been modified in the course of construction. In addition to the main body of the nave, there is an **aisle** along its northern side, which would have contained lesser altars, with a squat **bell tower** over its western bay.

The nave would have been separated from the choir by one or more screens, pierced by doorways, in front of which would have been the principal nave altar for the parish services of the lay folk. Although it is difficult to be certain, it appears that the earliest part of the nave is what remains of the arcade of four arches separating the nave from its aisle, running along the top of which was a clearstorey of high windows. Rather curiously, the southern wall is not parallel to the arcade, presumably because, for some reason, the original wall was rebuilt on a different line. A stub of wall protruding from the west wall shows its original position. Even more strange is the way the tower has been slotted into the bay at the west end of the aisle. Although the base course of the aisle wall suggests that the tower was intended by the time this wall was started, the tower fits very clumsily into the bay system defined by the inner arcade. However, it seems that the western arch of the arcade was walled up when the tower was built.

THE CHOIR

The choir was occupied by the canons during the long hours of their services. Their wooden seats, or stalls, would have been placed along the side walls of the western part of the choir, and for this reason the paired windows were placed at a relatively high level. The stalls would also have run across the choir against the rood screen, which separated the choir from the nave leaving space for a central doorway.

The **east end** of the choir was the most sacred part; it was the **presbytery**, and it housed the high altar and the ceremonial area around it. To give emphasis to this main altar of the church, the presbytery was lit by larger windows than elsewhere in the choir, the most prominent of which was the magnificent **east window**, with five tall lancets within a containing arch. A carved human head can be seen at the upper junction of two of the lancets. On the south side of the presbytery are a number of features provided to facilitate and enhance the celebration of mass at the adjacent high altar. Most prominent are the three moulded arches of the *sedilia*, or **seating recesses**, where the celebrant and his assistants sat at certain points of the services. To the east of this is a trifoliate-headed *piscina*, or **basin**, in which the priest washed the sacred vessels used during the mass. Yet further east is a small **aumbry**, or cupboard, in which some of those vessels might have been stored. Even in their weathered state, these fixtures give a glimpse of the original splendour of the presbytery and choir when they were more fully furnished, at which time the walls would have been plastered and painted, and the windows filled with coloured glass.

The interior of the choir viewed from the nave.

The sedilia *on the south side of the choir, within which the celebrating priest and his assistants sat during parts of the services.*

There are **doorways in the flanking walls** between the presbytery and choir. That on the south appears to have been the entrance to the choir which the canons would have used at the night-time services. A lean-to corridor ran along the outside of this wall, the roof supports for which still survive, and it probably connected with a stair from the dormitory on the upper floor of the adjacent range. The northern doorway opened into the **sacristy** within which the canons celebrating mass prepared themselves, and where the costly vestments and vessels used during the services would have been stored. The sacristy floor is now well below its original level, and only its lower walls survive. It was a lean-to building which initially abutted only the central third of the choir, but which, on the evidence of the roof supports, was later extended westwards to adjoin the north aisle of the nave.

There are **commemorative wall-plaques and graveslabs** in the choir, many of them inscribed to members of the Graham family. Buried here, alongside his wife, is the famous writer, traveller and politician, R B Cunninghame Graham, co-founder of the Scottish Labour Party in the 1880s and in 1928 the first President of the Scottish National Party.

The Priory as a Monastic Home

THE CLOISTER

The cloister consisted of an open area or garth around which the church and main domestic buildings of the priory were grouped. In their present form these buildings appear to be considerably later than the main body of the church and, although it is difficult to be certain of their date, they could be as late as the fifteenth century. They presumably replaced an earlier group of buildings, some foundations of which have been discovered around the walls of the refectory. Whilst these foundations indicate that the earlier buildings were parallel or at right angles to the main body of the church, the later ranges were set out in relation to the south wall of the nave and are therefore at an irregular angle to the rest of the church.

A view of the cloister. The south wall of the church is on the left, and the chapter house is in the middle. In the foreground are the foundations of the west cloister range.

THE EAST CLOISTER RANGE

The dormitory for the canons ran along much of the upper floor of the east range, with the **night-stair** probably at the north end and the remains of the **day-stair** at the south-east corner of the cloister.

The east cloister range and the choir from the south-east.

The chapter house viewed from the south cloister walk.

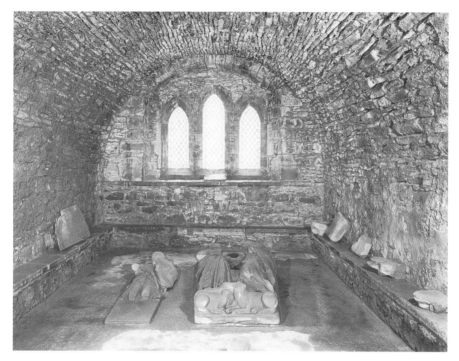

The interior of the vaulted chapter house, the meeting room of the canons. Around the wall are the benches on which they sat.

In its present state the most conspicuous part of the east range is the **chapter house**, which has been recently re-roofed. This was the daily meeting room of the community, and took its name from the way in which, in houses of Benedictine monks, a chapter of the monastic rule was read before meetings. It was also the place where the community discussed its business affairs, and within which the canons confessed their sins and received absolution. Like the rest of the ground floor of the range, the room was covered by a stone vault, and it was furnished with a stone bench around its walls. The lofty gables which now give it prominence are not original but date from its transformation into a mausoleum for the post-Reformation earls of Menteith. Traditionally this is said to have been done to receive the body of Lord Kilpont, the son of the seventh earl of the Graham line, who was murdered in the camp of his kinsman, the marquis of Montrose, in 1644. The recess above the doorway was designed to hold an armorial panel.

The effigy of an armed knight of the Stewarts.

The chapter house now contains a number of effigies and gravestones, brought here from the church for their protection, as well as pieces of carved and moulded stone which once decorated the priory buildings. The finest of these is the charming **double effigy** of Walter, the first earl of the Stewart line, who died in about 1295, and of his countess, Mary (see the illustration on page 7). Although badly weathered, its quality is still clear. There are fragments of two other effigies, one of which depicts an armed knight with the arms of the Stewart family on his shield. Of rather lesser quality is the fourteenth-century graveslab of Sir John Drummond, who is shown carrying a spear and shield (this stone is now mounted upright on the wall, but it would originally have lain flat over the grave). Drummond's family were

The graveslab of Sir John Drummond.

important benefactors of the priory, and his father, Sir Malcolm, gave it his estate of Cardross in thanks for his release from English captivity. To either side of Sir John's head are low relief carvings of a bishop standing on a serpent, and of St Michael slaying the dragon.

Mounted on the wall on the other side of the doorway is another effigy, but it is so worn that only the crossed legs and inturned feet can now be seen. Among the fragments is part of a graveslab with a very fine interlaced cross and the upper part of a sword with its hilt. Two of the architectural fragments are carved with human faces.

South of the chapter house is a **slype**, or passage, from the cloister to the area to its east, where the canons' cemetery may have been situated. This passage possibly also served as a parlour where discussion was allowed.

Much of the rest of the east range's ground floor is occupied by the calefactory or **warming house** with its large double fireplace. The warming house was the only room to have a fireplace at which the canons could warm themselves in cold weather. This room also has a sink or slop basin with a drain in its east wall, and it has been suggested that, although it would be unusual in this position, the room could have served as a kitchen. A more usual position for the kitchen would be beyond the refectory.

Tacked on to the southern end of the range is the undercroft of the reredorter or latrine block; access to the reredorter itself was from the dormitory above. The drain empties into a sump outside.

All of the buildings of this range were connected by the east cloister walk. But, rather unusually, on both the east and west sides of the cloister, the walks were wholly or partly absorbed within the body of the range instead of being built as lean-to pentices as was more usual. There were parallels for this arrangement at two other Augustinian houses: at Inchcolm, another island site, where the walks occupied the entire ground floor of three ranges, and in the rebuilt south range at Jedburgh. In England this type of arrangement was most commonly found in houses of friars.

Part of a graveslab with an interlaced crosshead and a sword.

THE SOUTH AND WEST CLOISTER RANGES

The **south range** was devoted to the refectory or **dining hall**, of which very little now remains. Although it appears to be contemporary with the other domestic buildings around the cloister as they now stand, it has been the second structure to occupy this site, and foundations of its predecessor may be seen to its west and south.

Like its counterpart on the south, very little remains of the **west range**; but there is enough to show that, as on part of the east side of the cloister, the walk must have been embodied within the range. The narrow section of the range which was not occupied by the walk was probably allocated to the cellarer of the priory for storing the produce which would be eaten in the adjacent refectory. The use of the destroyed upper floor cannot be known with certainty, but the way in which a stair is provided to it from the cloister may suggest that it was the prior's lodging. Such a position was often chosen for the residence of a community's head because it was sufficiently a part of the main body of the priory for the prior to take part in communal life, whilst it was also at the point at which the buildings were in closest contact with the outside world.

Further Reading

ON THE PRIORY:
W M Stirling *Notes, Historical and Descriptive on the Priory of Inchmahome* (1815)
D MacGibbon and T Ross *The Ecclesiastical Architecture of Scotland, vol 2* (1897)
J A Stewart *Inchmahome and the Lake of Menteith* (1933)

ON SCOTTISH MONASTERIES GENERALLY:
R Fawcett *Scottish Medieval Churches* (1985)
R Fawcett *Scottish Abbeys and Priories* (1994)

ON MARY QUEEN OF SCOTS:
D Breeze *A Queen's Progress* (1987)